Black Nomad

SUDAN INTERIOR MISSION

Founder: Rowland V. Bingham

The Sudan Interior Mission was founded in 1893 for the purpose of evangelism in Africa's Sudan—the area south of the Sahara, between the basins of the Niger River and the Nile.

The SIM is evangelical, international, and interdenominational. It has over 1300 missionaries serving in Liberia, Ghana, Dahomey, Upper Volta, Niger, Nigeria, Sudan, Ethiopia, Somalia, Aden (South Yemen), and Lebanon.

The SIM's ministry of preaching the gospel and establishing well-taught, indigenous churches is maintained by the freewill offerings of God's stewards.

SUDAN INTERIOR MISSION

United States:
164 West 74th Street, New York, N.Y. 10023

Canada:
405 Huron Street, Toronto 5, Ontario

United Kingdom:
84 Beulah Hill, London S.E.19, England

Australia:
59 Prospect Road, Summer Hill, N.S.W.

New Zealand:
Institute Place, 427 Queen Street, Auckland 1

South Africa:
Box 3017, Cape Town

Europe:
Chemin du Devin 95, 1012 Lausanne, Switzerland

Black Nomad

The story of Adamu Dogon Yaro,
messenger to West Africa's Fulani

by

EVA DOERKSEN

Author: *Black Gems for His Crown*
Polly Parrot

The Sudan Interior Mission

MCMLXIX

Published by Sudan Interior Mission
Library of Congress Number 69–20031

Printed and bound in England by
Hazell Watson & Viney Ltd
Aylesbury, Bucks

Introduction

The words in this book tell the true experiences of a Nigerian and his wife who were willing to be made "all things to all men that they might by all means save some."

Most of the incidents recorded here were told me by Adamu himself. I only wish it were possible to tell you in English the way he told them to me in Hausa.

I first met Adamu, or Dogon Yaro, as he was then called, in the Kagoro Bible School. He came one night to ask if he might carry my lantern and book to the church for prayer meeting. When he returned to escort me a few minutes later, the chimney globe had been washed and polished and every bit of dust wiped off the lantern.

As we walked along the railroad track he told me that he was a Fulani. My heart gave a jump. For a number of years I had prayed that there might be a convert among the Fulani who would in time carry the gospel to his own people, 6,000,000 of them scattered throughout West Africa.

Here was the answer to my prayer, a real live Fulani man with long legs and arms, walking in front of me! And he was a student in the Bible School!

How God used a Muslim *malam*, a lion, and two teen-agers to bring this man to Christ is all part of this true story.

Eva Doerksen

*To two fellow-soldiers, Kay Herring and Ruth Webb,
this book is affectionately dedicated*

Contents

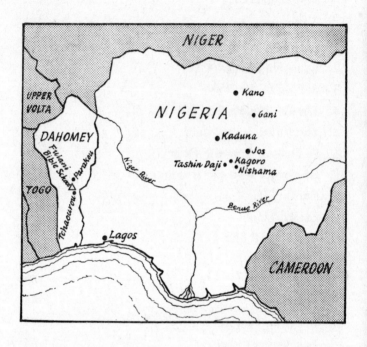

1. Fifth Son

Musa's dark eyes shone with pride as he glanced down at the freshly shaved head of his seven-year-old boy. Adamu, his fifth son, was to be a religious teacher, a *malam* like himself. The older boys could look after the cattle, but Adamu would bring great honor to Musa's name. He would follow in his father's steps.

Today Musa was taking his son to the distant Koranic school. Here Adamu would memorize the holy Koran and learn the rigors of being a disciple of the prophet Muhammed, a worshiper of Allah through the glorious faith of Islam.

A noisy group of relatives and neighbors, including Adamu's bosom playmate, Ibrahim, had gathered to bid them farewell. The Fulani, tall and slender, were quite different from other Nigerian tribes. They had fine features, thin lips, and long, narrow noses. Most of them were dressed in homespun garments. The younger boys wore large leather aprons decorated with cowrie shells.

Musa's pride was contagious as Adamu climbed on the waiting donkey's back. Taking up a small bundle and his long, smooth shepherd's stick, Musa shouted a final "Till I come back," and father and son exited grandly from the village.

Musa wore the customary *malam's* garb, a long, flowing robe and baggy trousers. On his head was a turban covered by a wide-brimmed hat made of soft grass. A pair of cowhide sandals completed his attire.

Adamu wore only a loincloth and a loose-fitting garment made of narrow strips of homespun cotton. A cloth cap covered his smooth-shaved head.

The path led over the hills, then dropped into nearly dry streambeds. Then it passed through the ripened fields of tall guinea corn, cotton fields waiting to be picked, and the empty peanut patches, whose fruit had long since been gathered in.

The child was full of questions. He loved his father, yet was afraid of him—a shy reverence African children have for their elders. But, somehow, today was different. Adamu was going away to school, they were alone, and his father was not too busy to talk.

"Baba," he asked, "my mother, the one who gave me birth—how was she?"

"She was good to look upon. She is no more. Death swept her away four years ago. You were only three years old then."

"Did she love me, Baba?"

"She wanted you very much. It was her desire, too, that you should become a servant of Allah."

"Did you have a naming feast for me, like Uncle Adamu did for his new son last month?"

"Of a truth we did," said the father. "We had a big feast for you. We feasted and danced for seven days. You were my little Dembo, my fifth son. Allah was good to me; He gave me five sons. I thanked Allah then, and I thank Him now."

Adamu lapsed into silence, his mind dwelling on the recent naming day ceremonies. As was the custom in the Fulani tribe, the little cousin had been circumcised the eighth day, his head was shaved, and he was given his name. After the religious ceremony, the feasting began.

Food consisted of large hunks of mutton and beef, as well as *hura da non*, made of large balls of guinea corn flour and water. These dough balls were broken into huge calabashes of buttermilk. This soupy substance was drunk with loud slurping noises from a gourd spoon passed from mouth to mouth. And, as always, there was *tuwo*, made by stirring guinea corn flour into boiling water. This mush, when done, was deftly formed into loaves and served with a thick gravy, hot with pepper.

When everyone had eaten his fill, the drummers started and the young people flung themselves into the dance. The young Fulani girls bounced and swayed to the rhythms, rows of bright beads around their necks. Brass ornaments dangled from their hair and ears. Brass rings adorned arms and ankles, jingling as they danced. Their blouses, and cloths tied around the waist to form a skirt, were made of bright silks and satins. The young men, too, were dressed in their finery. They wore long leather aprons decorated with cowrie shells. Their long, jet black hair was worn in tight braids sticking out in all directions. Dancing came naturally to these slim, lithe bodies.

Adamu, although too young to participate in the dancing, had enjoyed the feast. To have more than enough to eat was a rare treat. He watched his brothers with pride as they danced. When tired of watching the dance, he would find a secluded spot and listen to the older men as they sat in groups, discussing cows, money, and women.

Or he would watch the women, busy in the preparation of food, as they laughed and chatted, bending over the smoky fires.

To think that there had been a naming day feast like that for him!

"Why did you call me Adamu?"

"It is the name Malam Sulai whispered in your ear when the barber had finished shaving your head. I called you Gani because you were born at that season of the year. And does not everyone call his fifth son Dembo? Now don't forget to tell the teacher that your name is Adamu Gani," admonished the father.

The sun was almost blinding. "How many nights

before we reach the school, Baba?" asked the child as he wriggled on the donkey's back.

"Our journey will consume six nights before we reach the place, if God wills."

Reaching a small stream, Adamu slid off the donkey and waded in the cool water. After washing his hands, he cupped his right hand and dipped from the stream to drink.

Malam Musa filled his prayer kettle from the stream. He took from his bundle a small mat upon which he seated himself, and began *salla*, the prayer ritual. He was a strong and devout Muslim, the religious leader and teacher of his village.

The lad, too, left the coolness of the stream and sat down to recite his prayers as his father had taught him. Whenever he heard his father's voice raised to a high pitch, giving out the prayer call, Adamu was accustomed to leave his play, and run to the little circle of stones that marked out the prayer place.

Sitting on the ground with his legs folded in front of him, Adamu would repeat the Arabic sentences, then prostrate himself until his forehead touched the ground. He did this three times, and then spread out his hands toward heaven, palms upward, and repeated the prayer that invoked the blessing of Allah and asked His protection.

Prayers over, the father dipped guinea corn flour from a small bag tied to the donkey's back, and mixed it with water from the stream to make a thin gruel. Soon their lunch was ready. The two took alternate slow sips until the calabash was empty. Musa lifted his son onto the donkey and they resumed their journey.

Darkness found them in a small village, where they prepared to spend the night. Adamu dipped hungrily into the *tuwo da miya* that was offered to them. He wanted to listen to the men of the village as they sat around the dying embers of the cooking fire, but he was too weary. Dreams of home and his friend Ibrahim overpowered the quiet tones of the men's talking.

The next day, after early morning *salla* and warmed-over *tuwo da miya*, they were on their way. The traveling days furnished little variety. Each held the stops for *salla*, the small wayside markets, the occasional bath in a cool stream, the hot and dusty road, and the weariness at the end of the day.

"Baba," Adamu asked one day as he thought of his friend, now many miles behind them, "why must I go away to school? Why could not you teach me?"

"Af! My son, you would be good for nothing. You must have discipline. It is best that you go away. You will become a great *malam*. You will be the most respected person in the village. You will learn books, you will learn how to mix medicine and make leather charms to sell. Ever since you were born it has been my desire that you should become a servant of Allah."

2. Books and Beggars

Adamu sat quietly on the ground beside his father while arrangements were made with the Koranic teachers. To show any emotion would have brought derision from the other students, as well as a sharp rebuke from his father.

"Can the boy read?" the teacher asked his father.

"I have taught him myself to see some of the letters," assured the father. "And he knows many verses from the Koran by memory."

Adamu's heart warmed at the pride in his father's voice. He remembered how tedious it had been to sit as his father taught the village school-children. But now it was worth it.

Malam Musa left the next morning after giving the sum of two pounds to the teacher as payment for teaching his son. Neither parents nor school furnished the food. For that the boys must beg.

The young lad soon adjusted to his new life. Unless it was raining, classes were held outside, the pupils sitting in a circle around an open fire. Before long Adamu could shout as loud and as monotonously as the rest of them when they repeated their lessons. The confusion did not seem to disturb the boys when each one repeated a different portion out loud at the same time.

The early morning lesson over, the boys were divided into groups for their daily tasks. Some were sent to the stream for water, others went for firewood. Then there was the daily grinding. How the boys hated it! That was women's work. But it must be done if they were to have their supper of *tuwo da miya*. Down on their knees they went, rubbing a small stone over a large flat one, with the guinea corn between. The flour wasn't as fine as mother made it, and the *tuwo* was lumpy, but this was a man's world.

Each day a group of boys was sent out to solicit food. Dressed in rags and carrying calabashes, they went from house to house, singing a little beggar song. A handful of peanuts here, a measure of grain there, a chicken, a hunk of mutton, or a bit of salt, all were given in hope of a reward in the hereafter.

Adamu soon learned from the older boys how to play the clown by making himself look like an old man.

Walking in a bent-over position, leaning on a stick, with cotton stuck on his face to represent whiskers, he drew laughter from the crowd and gifts into the calabash. But in spite of these gifts the boys often went to bed hungry.

His first year at the school passed quickly. School provided stimulation for Adamu which was new and satisfying. He had never been really at home among his own outdoor people. He was thin. He was tall. Nomad he was by birth, but not by temperament. As he began to wrestle with ideas, he came alive. Somehow he felt at ease.

He looked forward to the visits of his father. Malam Musa always brought with him a gift, either food or a new garment. During one visit he gave his son a charm consisting of a small leather case which enclosed some "medicine." As he carefully fastened the charm to the boy's belt, he explained, "This will help you to learn faster."

Adamu's teacher, too, had a formula for making good students. After filling a wooden slate with Arabic writing, he washed it off, carefully saving the mixture of ink and water. This was given to the pupils to drink. Adamu was at first reluctant to drink the potion, but when he was assured that it would make him a better student, he obediently drank each time it was offered.

Adamu enjoyed his lessons and made rapid progress. In his second year he began writing lessons. The writing was done on a rectangular slate carved from soft wood, with a knot at the top for easy handling. He also learned to make ink by mixing powdered charcoal and gum arabic with water. Ink bottles grew on trees in the bush. A hard-shelled fruit resembling an orange, with a hole cut in the top and the seeds scooped out, made an excellent receptacle. Pens were carefully cut from thick-stemmed reed grass. Beginning at the right-hand side of his slate, and working toward the left, Adamu soon learned to form the graceful Arabic letters.

One year grew to two, and then three. Each year saw Adamu keenly interested in his studies, and storing every fact, every concept, in his fertile mind. After eight years of study Adamu, at 15, was well versed in the Koran and other ancient writings.

He had grown to a tall, lean boy, mostly arms and legs, and although his physique was occasionally smiled at, there was much respect for his grasp of the intellectual.

That year it was not his father who came to visit him, but his uncle Amadu. The uncle brought sad news. Adamu's father had died. Amadu had scarcely recovered from this initial shock when his uncle informed him that he must give up school and come home to herd cattle.

"But . . . the school," Adamu stuttered. "My studies! I am no herder of cattle! I . . . I . . . am . . . ."

His uncle's anger broke through the feeble pleas. The Fulani were cattle people. They had been cattle people for many generations. Adamu was a Fulani. He must come home.

3. A Lion in the Way

Adamu sat with his friend Ibrahim under the grotesque old baobab tree. Although eight years had passed since they had seen each other, it was not hard to pick up the threads of friendship.

"You will be staying home now, and we can be together," said Ibrahim.

"My uncle wishes me to stay home and help take care of the cattle," replied Adamu. "But I want to finish school. Another year, and I could be a *malam*. I cannot tend cattle. My heart does not desire it."

"But we could be together," repeated Ibrahim. "And

the initiation ceremonies are to be held in our village this year. You and I are old enough to enter."

"I do not wish to stay. I must finish school. It is all that I can think of."

"Your uncle will never let you go back to school."

They sat in silence for a while. Then Adamu spoke, "The hour is late. We must go to sleep. Promise you will not tell my uncle what I have said."

"I promise, my friend."

At first Adamu stayed near home, taking the cattle out each morning and bringing them back at night. Then came the dry season, and the cattle had to be taken farther afield. Adamu went with his older brothers, helped them make camp wherever they found a suitable spot, and slept with them in rough shelters. He had much time to meditate as he followed the herd at their grazing. At night the cattle were brought back to camp and put into an enclosure of thorn tree branches. The animals crowded around a smoky fire made to give them respite from mosquitoes and other stinging insects.

On one side of the herd slept the shepherd dog. On the other, in a very small shelter, Adamu and his brothers took their turn at spending the night. The watcher allowed himself little sleep. There was the constant threat that a leopard, lion, or hyena might carry off a calf or goat.

And while he watched, Adamu tried to think of a way to escape.

One day Adamu took the cattle out alone while his brothers went to market. The animals were feeding in a narrow valley between two rows of large, rocky hills.

Adamu, occupied by thoughts of the school that was denied him, did not notice for some time that the cattle had become restless. They sniffed the air and lowed, tossing their heads and pacing nervously. When he realized that something was wrong, Adamu looked around to find the cause. Suddenly a lion walked out of the thicket. The young lad stood for a moment, as though transformed into a wooden sculpture.

He had only his bow and arrow and his long shepherd stick. The momentary horror past, Adamu ran toward the beast, shouting and waving his stick. The cattle bolted. The lion, seeing the onrushing arms, legs, and stick, retreated into the bush.

Adamu stood, eyes fixed on the place where the lion had run. His breath was short, his long legs shook. The cry of his returning brothers as they rounded up the frightened cattle broke the spell of fear which had been cast over him.

When Adamu told the story around the campfire that night, he got little sympathy from his brothers.

"Why did you not kill the lion?" they asked. "You will never make a shepherd. You had better go back to your books."

"They are right," thought Adamu to himself. "I had better go back to my books."

It was Adamu's turn to keep watch that night. He could not dismiss the lion from his mind, nor did he feel that he could ever take the cows out again. Before the day dawned, his mind was made up. Herding the cattle and chasing lions was not to be his lifework.

"I'm going home for a few days," he told his brothers as soon as they began to stir.

"It's the lion," agreed the brothers among themselves.

Back in his village Adamu confided to his friend Ibrahim that he would soon run away from home and return to school. A few days later, gathering together his meager belongings, he slipped away while the rest of the family was still asleep.

Traveling the trail alone was not as exciting as Adamu had imagined. Strangers seemed more threatening than they had when he was with friends. Food seemed harder to find. A few days on the trail and the school seemed farther away than closer.

And so, when a traveler, seeing the boy on the road alone, asked Adamu where he was going, and then told him he could not possibly get to the school by himself, Adamu was ready to turn around and return home.

But the closer home he got, the stronger grew the thoughts of herding cows. And lions! And his uncle's bad temper and beatings.

He could not face it. When his traveling companion was sound asleep one night, Adamu slipped out quietly, and started back in the direction of the school once again.

He had been traveling for several days, when he stopped at a market place for food.

He was startled by a tap on the shoulder, and turning, recognized a distant cousin, now a police officer in the district. Adamu was overjoyed at the familiar face, and soon he was indiscreetly telling his cousin the whole story of his schooling, his herding, and his escapes.

Once again authority moved in on Adamu, and before he was completely aware of what was taking place, he found himself in the care of a group of men who were going to Adamu's village. They were to see that he arrived this time—official cousin's orders.

Less than a day's journey from his village as they stopped at an inn for the night, he kept his ears open. If only some traveler were going in the other direction! And then he heard them. Two men, and they were leaving early in the morning. The boy could not sleep. If he went home, it meant endless days of watching the cattle. And there were lions, and his uncle. Quietly he went to the other hut in the early morning and asked the men if he might go with them.

Adamu found himself among a group of people who were going to a place near Jos, in the west-central portion of Nigeria, to work in the tin mines.

Adamu's travels to and from his village finally pushed thoughts of going back to school from his mind, and, along with the others of the party, he applied for a job in the mines. The employer looked at the spindly boy and saw he was too frail to carry pans of dirt all day long. But he also saw in Adamu an unusual awareness, and offered to take him on as his personal servant. Adamu was content, and started work by looking after his master's horse.

But before long his new master, seeing the brightness of the boy and learning of his background, arranged for Adamu to resume his Islamic studies. His days became full ones, studying under the local *malam*, and earning his keep with the mine supervisor. His employer was a kindly man, who recognized the boy's total dependence upon him, and who treated him almost as an adopted son. Adamu, in turn, respected his master and responded with an intense loyalty.

Adamu was at home again in the world of thought and learning. He finished his studies and became a *malam*. Then he became a *limami*, the learned teacher of the village.

Five times a day, Adamu's voice rose above the clatter in the village as he called the faithful to prayer. Every Friday Adamu presided over the devotional services at the mosque. And it was Adamu who made the charms which many wore as protection against evil.

At last, Adamu had become what his father had wished. He was a spiritual leader of men. Adamu held his head high as he contemplated that he had stepped over every obstacle in his path, even lions, and had become the respected one. Allah had been good.

4. The Book with God in It

"Me? In charge of a railroad construction gang?"

Adamu could hardly believe his ears. All had been going smoothly, and then without warning, his employer reminded him that whatever else he was, he was still a servant. His master had taken a job with the new railroad which was opening Nigeria, and if Adamu wanted to continue working, he must leave with him, to be in charge of one of the work gangs.

Perhaps to ease the transition for Adamu, his master bought him a wife. And so it was that, in a small village near Kagoro, Adamu settled as a railroad supervisor's assistant.

Making friends had never been easy for Adamu. When friendship was offered by two boys who lived nearby, Adamu accepted gratefully. Though only in their teens, these boys were very much like Adamu in their interests. Adamu was surprised to find that they were students at the Sudan Interior Mission school in Kagoro.

"School was out early today," said Kure. "So we hurried to find you."

"What's that in your hand?"

"It's a book we want to read to you," said Abai.

Adamu took the book and leafed through it. It was Roman script, not the Arabic which he knew, and he wished he were able to read it. Then a question which had been growing with their friendship came out.

"Is God in your book?"

"Yes, He is," quickly answered Abai. "Listen, 'For God so loved the world, that he gave his only begotten son, that whosoever believeth in him should not perish, but have everlasting life.' "

"Show me the name of God on the page. I want to learn to read your book," said Adamu.

The boys left the Hausa New Testament with Adamu that night so he could compare it with the language he understood. Adamu's mind was once again awakened by the challenge of learning.

When the boys saw Adamu again they persuaded him to buy a primer. He mastered it in two weeks. Next they suggested that he buy a New Testament. But Adamu felt it was too much money. The boys offered to trade him a New Testament for his old primer, and Adamu accepted.

Then they struck a bargain with him. "We'll come to your house twice a week to teach you to read Roman script if you will teach us to read Aljemi script."

"That's a bargain," said Adamu. "But you must teach me to read first." In a few months' time Adamu was reading from the Hausa New Testament. As he read he became more and more convinced that what he was reading was the truth. A great struggle began in the tall Fulani. Often, in anguish, he would lay the book aside, determined never to open it again. But a heart hunger he had never before known made him pick it up again and again. He was convinced that Jesus was the giver of life, but how could he, a Muslim *malam*, change direction so drastically? If he confessed Christ, there was a price to pay. It meant turning his back on his Islamic religion entirely.

His young teachers tried to help him. Once he promised that he would go to church with them. But when he reached the church, he lacked the courage to go in. He stood at the open window and listened. After a week of painful internal struggle, he went again and this time he entered, but sat near the door so he could get out quickly. The conflict between what he had been taught and what he was beginning to believe once again proved too strong. Adamu ran from the church before the service was over.

His young friends, who usually attended services at school, now offered to go with him and to sit with him in church. On the Sunday that the boys and Adamu came, the missionary was speaking from the text "For all have sinned and come short of the glory of God."

The missionary spoke with much fervor, frequently raising his voice for emphasis. Adamu left the church hurriedly.

Abai, running, caught Adamu. "Wait! Wait, Adamu!"

"It is not good. I cannot stay."

"But why?"

"If your God is as angry as His messenger, He will have nothing to do with me."

But his young friend was also sensitive.

"God is not angry, Adamu," he said quietly. "There are those of His messengers who shout what He has told them, and, indeed, His words against sin are strong. But God is not angry."

As the voice of the missionary continued from the small church in the distance, Adamu listened to the quiet, open words of his friend. He heard of a God who not only hated sin, but hated its effect on His creation. He heard of a God who loved His creation so much that He died for it. He heard of a God who could, by the death of His Son, offer any man freedom from the guilt and power of sin.

The following Sunday, sitting between his two friends, Adamu managed to squirm through the entire service. The words, the songs, the faces about him, all combined to enforce in Adamu's mind what he already knew. At the close, Abai nudged him, "Stand up and ask the people to pray for you."

Tall, thin Adamu, Koranic teacher from the nomad Fulani tribe, stood up. With much feeling he said, "I believe in Jesus. I want you to pray for me."

5. The Voice in the Night

Adamu did not know it, but his new walk was to lead through strange pastures. For some time after his momentous decision his life continued much as usual. He followed many of his Islamic ways, unaware that better things were in store.

At night he took off his charms and carefully placed them around his sleeping mat, one on either side, one at his head, and the other at his feet.

One night, at midnight, he was suddenly awakened by someone in the room. He saw a man in white standing beside him.

"Can those charms protect you?" asked the man. "Do not *I* save? Those charms are nothing. If you were to die tonight, charms could not help you."

"Lord," Adamu stuttered in fear, "show me what You want me to do." As a Muslim, Adamu had repeated many prayers, but this was the first time he had prayed spontaneously.

"I want you to prove me. I want you to prove that I am your keeper. Put the charms away. Don't leave them in your house."

Adamu lay shaking with emotion. His wife awoke and asked what had happened. He told her and she asked, "Do not devils sometimes speak to people like that?"

Fearful, but determined to obey, Adamu gathered up his charms, took them to an outside kitchen, and hid them in the grass roof. He went to work the next day without them. To his amazement, nothing happened!

A few weeks later his wife found the charms. Greatly agitated, she gathered them up and ran to where her husband was working on the railway.

Afraid he might die even before she got the charms to him, as soon as she was within hearing distance, she held them up and shouted, "You have done a great forgetting! Come quickly and get them!"

"I put them there, take them back."

She looked at him, speechless, then went slowly back to the house. "If you want to die," she mumbled, "that's your affair."

As the days passed, Adamu's smile and faith grew brighter. "I know now that God is my keeper. I have tried Him for three weeks without charms. No evil has befallen me. I want to do whatever the Lord shows me."

At the church, he made public the way God had worked with him, and his faith strengthened. But more tests were on the way.

It came time for Ramadan, the annual Islamic fast which is observed during the daylight hours for one full month. For a true Muslim to fail to keep this fast is believed to be certain disaster. Adamu, as *limami*, would be expected to have charge of the ceremonies.

But Adamu's break with the past had been complete, and to the chagrin and anger of his Muslim wife and friends, he neither kept the fast nor presided at the ritual events. His new Christian behavior was beginning to alienate all with whom he had once known friendship. And although his had never been a personally involved marriage, the increasingly angry attacks of his wife began to weigh heavily on his mind.

Then one night another voice woke him. "Quit your work and go to Kagoro Bible School that you may learn to teach others." The voice was warm and familiar, and Adamu was determined to obey his Lord no matter what.

"You are determined to shame me and become a traitor to your people!" His wife's angry voice sliced the air. "You are nothing but an unbeliever! A *kafiri*, an apostate! Do not expect me to accompany you in this folly. I will stay right here!"

His employer had always been more sympathetic. "At the end of six months, if you want to come back, your job will be open for you. On the other hand, if you want to give up your job for good, you have my blessing."

Once again Adamu was "at home" in school. He was studying, and his mind came alive with the enjoyment of it. The classes and the fellowship of other believers lifted him during the week, but then the weekends came, and he had to return home.

"*Kafiri! Kafiri!*" his wife shouted, and grew harder in her opposition.

It was as though he led two lives, one full and exciting, the other shrill and stabbing. He prayed. His fellow students prayed. Missionaries from Kagoro had many long conversations with his wife, hoping to show her the truth.

One day, to Adamu's despair, but not to his surprise, the situation was settled. His wife, seeing that she would never win him back, demanded a divorce. The authorities granted it, and she left, never to see him again.

Adamu was free now, to serve and to study, but his situation was marred by the divorce. He had a humble spirit and did willingly and well the most menial of tasks. He had a keen sense of humor and liked best telling jokes on himself. But he was often lonely. All the other young men at the Bible School were from pagan tribes, from backgrounds different from his own. After years of married life it was not easy to look after the cooking of his own food, a task completely relegated to the women. His wife, though incompatible, had provided certain natural satisfactions, and the possibilities of getting another wife seemed nil. He knew of no Christian girls among the Fulani, and a Christian girl from a pagan tribe, he reasoned, would not wish to marry him. So the months passed by, with Adamu looking to God each day for help and strength and guidance.

During his last year in Bible School, Adamu had a dream in which he saw a multitude of men and women who were dying in their sins. He was filled with concern for them and felt he must go and tell them the remedy for sin.

He thought of the dream again and again, more convinced than ever that God was calling him to preach the gospel. But where? Unmarried, he could not go to Hausa country, or even to his own people. They would not accept him, a man with no wife. Nearer home were only pagan tribes and they, he felt, would not want a Fulani nomad to preach to them. Tribal differences were too strong.

Where did God want him to serve?

6. In Danger from the Dodos

In one section of the Kagoro district was a large pagan tribe practically untouched by the gospel. Strong of body and wild in nature, these Kagoros spent their days in farming and hunting. Fetishism was to them no empty ritual. Spirit worship was deeply imbedded in their nature. The fetish priest ruled the tribe. Fetish huts dotted the countryside. These round mud huts, measuring about ten feet in diameter, were built with low walls and a grass roof that came to a sharp peak in the center. Inside were sacred ritual pots, skulls of animals captured in their hunts, and human skulls.

The tribe observed many feasts during the year, always accompanied by drinking and dancing. It was not unusual for a dance to continue three days and nights without a break. Dodos, or spirit men, were everywhere. These were men from the local tribe dressed in hideous costumes which completely hid their identity. Weird-looking creatures, they went about at night frightening women and children and demanding food. Terror accompanied their movements. The women firmly believed, as they had been taught from childhood, that these men were the spirits of their dead relatives come back to visit them.

The dodos gathered in the sacred groves and fetish huts, sometimes as many as 200, to perform the tribal rites of blood sacrifices.

Before the coming of the English, the Kagoro tribe was feared because the men were headhunters. They drank their beer, dedicated to evil spirits, from human skulls. Headhunting was long since forbidden, yet no outsider knew what went on when the dodos were having a gathering in one of their fetish huts. The huts were considered sacred, and only men dedicated to fetish worship were allowed inside. Strangers traveling alone through that part of the country were known not to have reached their destination. The fetish priest needed only to blow his weird-sounding whistle, night or day, and men came running from all directions to do his bidding.

It was to Tashin Daji, a small village in this tribe, that Adamu came. This was to be his first parish. It would be a difficult one. Adamu was unmarried, he was from another tribe, and he was the representative of another religion.

Alone, he gathered materials and built his house. Alone, he dug a well. Alone, he prepared and ate his food. While he worked, he spoke with those who came to watch. There was little response from the villagers. The language barrier was difficult, and they were suspicious of the stranger.

Awakening one night, he felt something cold beside him. Carefully turning, he saw a large snake sharing his sleeping mat. Another night he was awakened by a crackling noise overhead. He jumped up and reached the door just in time to escape being injured as the roof caved in over his bed. The Lord was proving to Adamu that He was his keeper.

Returning home one day from preaching, he had to ford a swollen stream. Wading through the water he lost his balance. The boiling current carried him downstream, tumbling him over and over and throwing him against the rocks. Adamu was able to save himself by catching hold of a low branch. But he had lost his clothes in the struggle. He sat down until dark, then walked the eerie night trail home.

Adamu's heart was often heavy at the depravity of the people around him. He saw them take the finest of their goats and chickens and offer them as sacrifices to evil spirits. The blood was sprinkled on long stones stuck upright into the ground, or on broken pots—anything that had been dedicated by the fetish priest as an altar.

"Why," asked Adamu one day after he had a better grasp of their language, "do you offer the blood?"

"We do not want the spirits to be angry with us and kill our children. We must bring these sacrifices to appease them. And our crops—we do not want the spirits to withhold our food."

"But the living God is not like that," said Adamu. "He loves you, He sent His only Son . . . ."

He was not allowed to finish. "We will not listen to that. That is the white man's religion. We are following what our fathers taught us."

"But I am not a white man, yet I follow the God of love."

"You ate the white man's food! He bewitched you! We do not want your words. This is the road our fathers and grandfathers followed. We shall follow it too."

Time after time Adamu was turned away. If only he could make them understand.

But not all turned a deaf ear to the message Adamu brought. There was the old man in the village who was dying the slow death of leprosy. Adamu found him ready to listen, and when he finished telling him the story of the One who came to save, the old man said, "Now tell me again so I won't forget."

As Adamu spoke to him again and again, the darkened heart was enlightened and the weary soul found rest in Christ. He died rejoicing.

The old man had two sons who witnessed their father's death. They were so impressed that they came

to Adamu later and asked to hear the words that had
made such a difference in their father.

And there was his next-door neighbor, who from the
very first had been friendly. He had shared much of
Adamu's new life in the village, and eventually grew
in understanding of Adamu's message.

There were, too, the four young men who came
almost every evening to Adamu that he might teach them
to read. The seed so faithfully sown began to bear fruit.
By the time he had been there four years Adamu had
gathered around him a little company whose faith was
in Christ.

Then came another time of discouragement—the
tribal initiation ceremonies, a major feast held once
every seven years. At this time boys around the age of
16 were dedicated to the evil spirits and initiated into
the rites of fetish worship. After participating in these
rites, the boys were looked upon as men. They paid
taxes and began to think seriously of marriage.

Adamu's heart was troubled as he saw how eagerly
the boys looked forward to this event. Even the boys
who had been coming to the services and reading classes
seemed powerless to resist the pull of the initiation
ceremonies.

The boys were taken to a hidden sacred grove up in
the hills. There among the trees and thick brush they
were kept for a month while the older men instructed
them. When they returned to the village, they were no
longer innocent boys, and many had lost interest in
Adamu's message.

One day not long after the initiation ceremonies,

Adamu found it necessary to take a trip to the railroad town about 12 miles away. He decided to make the trip at night and avoid the heat of the day. The moonlit path led past many fetish huts and spirit groves. Reaching a small village along the way, Adamu felt too sleepy to go on. To ask for a place to sleep would be very dangerous, but vegetation was too dense to venture sleeping out in the open. As he was trying to decide what to do, he noticed a fetish hut by the side of the road.

"Just the thing," thought Adamu. "I'll lie down in there, take a few winks, and be gone before anyone in the village is up."

He had just settled down when he was seized with coughing.

"Who's there?" shouted a startled voice from a nearby hut.

Adamu lay perfectly quiet, hardly daring to breathe. Things quieted down, but just as he was dozing off again, another uncontrollable cough seized him. This time the neighbor roused and came out. After looking all round, he glanced into the fetish hut. Adamu was discovered. The air was shattered by the weird shriek of the dodo whistle and within minutes Adamu found himself surrounded by an angry mob, all talking at once.

Adamu could not understand all that was being said, largely because the village had its own dialect, but he heard enough to know that the men were planning to kill him. Escape was impossible. The fetish priest stepped into the hut.

"Who are you? Where do you come from? Where are you going? Who sent you?" he hurled at him in quick succession.

"I live in Tashin Daji," Adamu answered. "I'm a servant of the living God. My Master has sent me." Then, mainly to reassure himself, he added, "I know my God is able to keep me."

"Who is your god?" asked the fetish priest disdainfully. Then he added, "If a white man has sent you, then you must have a letter."

Adamu thought quickly. He pulled an old letter out of his bag. None of the men was able to read, but the letter was passed from hand to hand and each man clicked his tongue knowingly and agreed that it was the hand of a white man.

"If a white man has sent him, he will soon send another messenger to find him. We will take him to the priest's house and keep him for three or four days, then if no one comes, we will kill him," they agreed among themselves.

"I refuse to go to the priest's house," said the prisoner, still using the Hausa language. "If you are going to kill me, kill me here and now."

After another heated discussion, it was decided to take him to a fetish hut farther up the hill, and end his life there.

When the mob reached the top of the hill, they pushed Adamu into the hut. He fell on his face and lay motionless, pretending to be hurt by the fall. After further discussion, they decided to wait until morning to take his life. A fire was built in the middle of the hut, and six men appointed to keep guard. The rest returned to their homes.

Still lying motionless, but silently praying for deliverance, Adamu watched the guards out of the corner of his eye. After a while he noticed that one of them had fallen asleep. Then another started breathing heavily. Eventually his bodyguard of six men were all asleep. "God is my keeper," Adamu sighed in gratitude. "Thank You, Lord. Thank You."

He rose silently, picked up his extra garment and books, and slipped cautiously over the sleeping forms.

He walked softly until he was out of earshot, and then ran through the thick underbrush. A sharp stick pierced his foot, but in his haste he paid little attention to it. He hurried through the remaining night hours. Early morning found him limping near a deep ravine over which a palm log had been thrown for a bridge. Exhausted, he sat down on a rock to rest. His foot was throbbing painfully. Examining it carefully for the first time, he discovered that the stick had broken off deep inside. The foot was so swollen that, try as he might, he was unable to get the stick out. He knew he must get to the mission for help. He stood, and collapsed. His muscles had cramped and he was unable to unbend his knee. The pain in his foot was extreme.

He sat for hours, waiting for someone to come along who could help him across the crude bridge and get to the mission. No one came. Finally, pushing himself along on his hands and buttocks, he managed to cross the log, and forcing himself to stand, despite the anguish, hobbled to the mission dispensary. It was many days before he was able to walk again.

But Adamu was restless. The soldier wanted to get back into the battle. As soon as he was able to walk, he took a Christian friend with him, and visited the village where his life had been threatened. The women gathered to listen to the preaching, but the men, recognizing Adamu, refused to come near. A young boy with round, frightened eyes, was heard to say, "There he is! That's the one! He's not human! He can make himself invisible!"

Then Adamu understood. The guards, ashamed to admit that they had gone to sleep, had told the village that Adamu was a spirit, and while they were sitting on guard, he had made himself invisible and disappeared.

Adamu continued his work at Tashin Daji, but his loneliness continued to press on his mind. "There are no Christian girls in my tribe," he confided to one of his missionary friends, "and a Christian girl from another tribe would not marry a Fulani."

One time, as his missionary friend was preparing to visit his own fiancée, he said to Adamu, "Why don't you come with me tomorrow and try to find a girl?"

Adamu gave him his usual answer, "A girl from another tribe would not marry a Fulani," and considered the matter closed. But that night he had a dream. A voice said to him, "If you go to Kagoro tomorrow with your friend, you will find a wife."

He awakened feeling almost guilty, thinking that perhaps Satan had put the thought into his mind. He asked the Lord to forgive him and fell asleep, only to dream the same thing again.

In the morning, Adamu was surprised as his friend said, "I dreamed last night that there is a girl waiting for you at Kagoro. Why don't you come with me?"

In Kagoro Adamu visited the African pastor, who was a friend of the local chief, a Christian. While they were chatting, the pastor remarked, "Adamu, I dreamed last night that you were going to marry the chief's sister. You and he know each other well. I'm sure if he knew you wanted her, he would let you have her."

"She would not have me," replied Adamu. "She will want to marry someone from her own tribe."

The pastor was not so easily convinced. "Will you give me permission to ask the chief?" he insisted. "He has been his sister's guardian since their father's death."

With Adamu's consent, Pastor Bagaiya took the question to the Christian chief. The chief was pleased. "It would give me great pleasure if Adamu married Jumai," he said. "I know he is a fine Christian man and will be good to her."

Adamu, the missionary, and the pastor smiled their satisfaction. Just one difficulty remained. Jumai was only a child. Adamu would have to wait until she grew up.

7. Encounter with the Headhunter

Adamu's influence continued to grow at Tashin Daji. His concern for the people, his clear presentation of the gospel, and his interest in individuals won the respect of many. When he had been there five years, he had achieved a great deal. Response during his fifth year had been very good. There was a large congregation, worshiping in a church they had built themselves. With this core of believers established, Adamu felt free to return to Kagoro Bible School for further study. Since he had left, educational standards had risen, and Adamu wanted to earn his certificate.

He returned to Kagoro and resumed studies. He continued to preach, going out on weekends to the nearby areas.

On one occasion, during a week's vacation from Bible School, Adamu was invited to accompany two lady missionaries on a visit to the Kabeni tribe. These wild tribal people of the hills had not been easily approached for the Lord. The first messenger to the Kabenis, an evangelist from the Yoruba tribe, was driven out by an angry mob. The love of Christ, however, constrained him to go back again to live and preach Christ among them. He died a few months later of a mysterious disease. But even in that short time the Word had taken root and there was a small group of Christians among the Kabenis in the lower hills. The two missionaries hoped to encourage these Christians as well as to visit some of the untouched villages higher in the hills. The more inaccessible the village, the more deeply rooted demon worship seemed to be. The Kabenis were reported to practice in secret their ancient headhunting rites, now banned by law.

Fortified by prayer, Adamu and the ladies started their climb. The Kabeni Christians, fearful of the notorious villages farther up, refused to go with them.

They were an odd-looking trio. One of the ladies was a short, very determined Scottish lassie. The other was built for comfort, not for speed. Although plump and easygoing, she was not at all lacking in determination. Adamu was tall and streamlined. Nature had been generous in the length of his arms and legs.

Walking into one of the villages they found the place

apparently deserted. An uncanny silence, still as death, pervaded the place. The inhabitants were obviously spirit worshipers. There was a fetish hut at the edge of the village. Tall stones stuck upright into the ground were streaked with drink offerings. Blobs of blood mixed with chicken feathers were plastered on either side of the entrances to the huts.

Sensing unseen eyes looking at them from behind mat doors and through cracks in the mud walls, the trio stopped and preached aloud to their invisible audience before moving on.

They climbed over more rocks and through more silent villages, until they reached the compound of the district chief. His was a village of raw pagans. There was not a piece of cloth as big as a handkerchief in the entire village. The women wore a few leaves; the men went around the way they had been born. The old chief was the only one who was clothed. He was dressed in a leather loincloth, with a leopard skin, front legs tied together, draped over one shoulder.

The party of three found the old man sitting in front of his hut sunning himself. He was droopy from too much beer, and his face, more animal than human, showed its years of debauchery. Adamu greeted him and, to make conversation, asked the road to Kabeni town.

Suddenly the inert figure came alive. Looking them over, he said, "You'll never get to Kabeni town tonight. It is much too far. You must stay at my house. Does anyone know you have come here? One, two, three heads. You must come into my house."

"Oh no, we cannot come in," said Adamu. "We want to tell you the news about God, then return to our homes."

"One, two, three heads," muttered the chief, one evil eye directed toward the plump lady. "You must spend the night at my house," he repeated in a louder tone.

"No, we must go back," insisted Adamu, taking in the situation. "But first we want to tell you about God. That is our reason for coming."

Adamu motioned to the ladies to move away while he kept the old chief's attention. But as they slipped away, the old scoundrel saw his prey trying to escape, and blew a whistle. As if by magic, men came running from all directions.

Adamu stayed just long enough to tell the chief and his men that God loved them, and then followed the ladies down the hill. They ran, heeding neither thorns nor rocks. But when they reached a little clearing, they were dismayed to find that the chief and his men, following another path, had arrived there ahead of them. Again the chief insisted that they spend the night in his village.

"There is a storm coming," objected Adamu. "See the rain clouds over the hills? We must make haste."

Climbing up to the top of a huge boulder with the alacrity of a wild goat, the old chief began waving his arms in the air and shouted, "I am the god of the rain! It cannot rain until I give my permission."

Not daring to run from the enraged headhunter, the two missionaries and their escort kept backing down the hill, saying, "Long live the king! Long live the king!"

With a frenzied leap the old chief was off the rock. "You are not leaving my village tonight!" Knees trembling, the trio raised their right arms as a token of respect to the chief and shouted with one voice, "Long live the king! We are on our way!"

They backed down the hill while an unseen force held the chief from following them. He stood there waving his arms and shouting, "I am the god of the rain. You are not leaving my village tonight!"

Finally, turning their backs on the enraged ruler, the trio took to their heels and fled. Down the hills they ran, not resting until they reached the safety of a little village some distance from the old chief and his men.

Their clothes were torn, their arms and legs were scratched, and one of the ladies had lost her shoe, but they had escaped the headhunters' pot.

8. Turning Point

Shortly before graduation, Adamu married his little
Jumai, the Kagoro Chief's sister. Life seemed to begin
all over again for him. So proud was Adamu and so
pleased with his young wife that he thoroughly spoiled
her. But Jumai became a true helper, and their marriage
was a happy one. It was a turning point in the life of
Adamu.

When Bible School was finished, Adamu and his
young bride were sent to Nishama, an outstation behind
the Kagoro hills. A wild tribe of demon worshipers,
they conducted their rituals in sacred places of the forest

instead of building fetish huts. The women wore only leaves with a narrow strip of cloth tied around their hips. The men wore small leather loin cloths. They were exceptional hunters, and it was not unusual to see them bringing home big game. When their prey happened to be a leopard or bush cow, the event was celebrated with a beer drink in which the whole village took part.

Adamu and Jumai set up their new little home in Nishama. Although there was sunshine in the home, and sunlight drenching the beautiful Kagoro hills in the distance, there was heavy cloud in the hearts of the people. Eventually the happy couple found four young men who expressed an interest in the gospel, but the rest of their neighbors were openly opposed, and plainly showed them that they were not wanted.

For a year, Adamu and Jumai met little but hostility and suspicion. Their home was like a tiny village within the larger one. Their relationship developed in closeness and mutual dependence as they found in each other what God was not yet pleased to give them in others. Even when Jumai was expecting her first child, it made little difference to the neighbor women, although such an event would normally have been a cause for friendly interest.

Then, soon after Jumai went back to her home in Kagoro to bear her first child, the situation changed. A man, working in his yard, greeted Adamu as he passed. Adamu answered the greeting and added, "You should repent of your sins, you know, and believe on the Lord Jesus."

"What do you mean saying that to me! Say that again, and you'll see what happens."

Adamu, a bit overzealous, repeated the words, "You should repent of your sins, and believe on Jesus."

The man rushed out, gave Adamu a blow on the face, and said, "Now say it again!"

Adamu took up the challenge, "You should repent and believe on the Lord Jesus that you might have eternal life."

Suddenly several men carrying clubs appeared on the scene. A year's worth of resentment went into the beating Adamu was given. After regaining consciousness, Adamu, bruised and aching, walked to Kagoro to report the matter. He was advised to take the words to the district head at Jama'a. That meant another long walk.

The district head, after hearing the report, had the men called. However, not wishing to favor the Christians, he told Adamu that he should not have called to the man in his own yard. He should have called him out and talked to him.

"But I did not wish to disturb the man in his work," replied Adamu.

The officer decided that each of the men would pay Adamu a fine. "But I do not wish them to be punished," Adamu interceded. "I really only want them to be warned. For my own injuries, I do not mind. But they must be more careful, or next time they may have a murder on their hands." He asked the officer again not to fine the culprits.

"All right," said the officer, "if you do not want the money, I'll keep it. But they must be fined."

The guilty ones were each required to pay five pounds and were sent home with a warning to be more careful about the use of their clubs.

It was not long before the whole village heard of Adamu's pleading that the men not be fined. This was hard to understand. They had been so antagonistic. They had beaten him. And he had asked that they only be warned.

The spirit of hostility was broken, and as the very men who beat him sought to be his friends, Adamu saw not only what he preached, but what he lived beginning to grow and multiply.

9. Closed Doors

The long green train sped through the bush, puffing its way to Kano, the largest city in the northern area of Nigeria.

Adamu settled his long legs as comfortably as possible, shifted on the hard wooden seat, and covered his face with his robe, pretending to be asleep. The passengers in third class were noisy and restless. There was shouting back and forth, and much commotion at every stop.

Adamu wanted to be alone with his thoughts. Although uncomfortable and weary, deep down he felt very happy. The thought of going to Kano gave him a sense of elation. The city, one of the oldest in Nigeria, was founded over a thousand years ago. He knew he would find hundreds of his own people, the Fulani, as well as many prominent Islamic religious teachers there. Ever since he had heard of the need in Kano, he had been praying for that city. Now he had been asked to come for three months to help in the Lord's work there. He smiled behind his robe in happy anticipation.

There was another thought that kept coming to the young preacher's mind. Was this perhaps to be his future field of endeavor? Would witnessing in Kano become his lifework? Was this perhaps the reason God had chosen him out of hundreds of Islamic teachers and brought him in contact with the gospel? Was this why his life had been spared so many times?

"Dear Lord, grant me an obedient heart to do Thy will," he prayed.

At the station, Adamu was met by the missionary. It was only midmorning, but the sun beat down upon them with burning heat. The two pushed their way through the crowd to the car.

"Have you ever been in Kano?" asked his new friend.

"I have never touched upon coming to Kano," said Adamu. "I am very happy to be here."

"I'll drive you around a bit," said the missionary. "Kano is divided into three sections. We'll go to the part called New Town first."

They passed rows and rows of small houses, many of them with large rooms across the front used for shops. Living accommodations were in the back. Here lived the "outsiders," mostly people from the southern tribes who had come to Kano as traders, carpenters, masons, and shopkeepers.

There were also better homes which housed the educated class of Kano. As they drove through the business section, Adamu was amazed at the large buildings and wide streets.

"Kano is like any modern city," explained his companion. "Large stores, shops, garages, factories, and business offices. Transcontinental jets land at the airport daily."

"I have never seen a ship of the sky on the ground," said Adamu. "I have only seen them like birds flying through the sky."

They drove through the European section, past residences with beautiful flower gardens, on and on through the city until finally the missionary pulled up at a large, low building.

"This is our Sudan Interior Mission eye hospital," said the missionary. People come here from many miles away. We have hundreds of patients at the clinic, in addition to bed patients. We would like you to help us by preaching in the clinic and hospital wards."

Adamu's heart warmed at the prospect. How different from Nishama—scores of people who could be approached with the gospel, who had reason to listen and consider the message!

"I'll introduce you to our staff and then take you to Pastor Alhamdu's home, where you may rest," said the missionary. Adamu was only partly aware of the introductions and the remainder of the ride. Islam was obvious everywhere. Adamu's heart pounded. "I know this so well," he thought. "And I have so much to do!"

"Rest from your tiredness," said the missionary as he left Adamu at the pastor's house. "Tomorrow I will have someone take you so you can see the real Kano, the ancient city inside the walls."

And the following morning they stood, Adamu and Pastor Alhamdu, at one of the gates in the ancient wall. Adamu clicked his tongue in amazement. "I did not know the walls were so high," he marveled.

"The history books tell us that Chief Gyimasu started building these walls over 800 years ago," explained Pastor Alhamdu. "They were built by slave labor. When they were new, they were 40 feet wide at the base, and in some places, as high as 50 feet. They are crumbling now. The rains of 800 seasons have washed away much of the earth, and the desert winds have blown away the sand. There are 11 miles of wall and 13 gates. This gate in front of us is the one through which the British entered when they conquered the city in 1903. Kano was one of the last cities of Nigeria to surrender. Some of the gates are so narrow there is barely room for a donkey to pass through."

He pointed to two ditches surrounding the wall on the outside. "That is where the earth for building the wall was taken. Then the ditches were planted with thorn bushes for extra protection from invaders."

"But is it not true," injected Adamu, a hint of tribal pride in his voice, "that in spite of thorn bushes, ditches, and walls, the Fulani people conquered this city nearly 600 years ago?"

Pastor Alhamdu nodded, and the two men walked into the city. This was the forbidden territory, where the very soil was sacred to Islam. There was a Christian witness in other sections of the city, but not here. Adamu's pulse quickened.

Cars, trucks, donkeys, bicycles, camels, pedestrians, dogs, and goats jostled each other in the labyrinth of ancient, narrow streets.

The flat-roofed houses, many of them two stories high, were built so close together they looked as if they might tumble into each other's windows.

Open sewers and stagnant water holes filled the city with stench and mosquitoes. Hoodlum children, begging for money and clothes, followed the strangers as they wound their way through the narrow passages between the houses. The two men did nothing but greet the people, but even so an air of antagonism met them wherever they went. Strangers were not welcome.

They walked past the chief's palace, a jumble of ancient and modern architecture. They passed through one of Kano City's nine large markets, where wares of every description lay spread out on the ground.

On their way out of the city they came to the new mosque. "This building," said Pastor Alhamdu, "is the largest of its kind in Nigeria. It was erected at a cost of many thousands of pounds."

On this Friday morning, as on every Friday, the mosque and the spacious courtyard were filled with worshipers.

The young preacher's heart ached as he watched the men slip off their sandals, walk into the building, and prostrate themselves on the cold cement floor, invoking the blessing of Allah.

He remembered how he, too, had worshiped in this way many, many times. Yet each time he had left the mosque without the peace he sought.

"They don't know, do they?" he said to Pastor Alhamdu, softly.

As they were leaving the city, they paused just outside the gate. "In all that multitude of people," asked Adamu, "is there not one who knows about the Lord Jesus and His saving power?"

"As far as we know, no," said the pastor. "And this task is ours. Europeans are not allowed to live inside the old city. They are not allowed to preach inside the walls. If these people are to hear the gospel, it must be from the lips of their fellow Nigerians."

Adamu had little to say as they walked home. The burden lay heavy on his heart. For over 500 years Islam had held complete sway in Kano City. And more formidable than the walls surrounding the city were the walls of antagonism around the hearts of its people.

Adamu busied himself in his work. The time passed quickly, and he found great joy in those who responded to his witness in the hospital. There was an indescribable satisfaction in seeing his Fulani fellows listen intently as he explained the gospel story. Something stirred within him, a feeling that this citadel of Islam would not let him go.

He returned to Jumai and his work at Nishama after three months, but he could not forget his own people in Kano, so badly in need of the gospel.

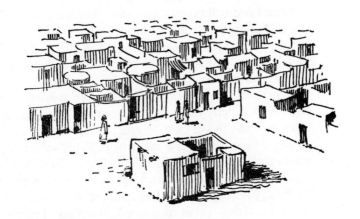

10. The Cursed Site

Adamu read the letter again and again. Then he called his wife. "Jumai," he began slowly, "it is from Kano. They want us to come. They feel the time is ripe to attempt a witness inside the ancient walls. They want us to begin it."

"Where would we live?" asked his wife.

"We would need a house inside the walls."

"Inside?" Jumai questioned, a hesitant note in her voice. "They will not listen to us. They will hate us."

"That is not new to us," Adamu replied. "God seems to have been getting us ready for this task. Do you not remember our first year here at Nishama?"

"I do not care about myself," Jumai responded, "but little Musa . . . suppose they do something to our son?" she said, hugging her first-born.

"The Lord will take care of him. And us. I feel this is the call of God. We must obey."

Adamu decided it would be best for him to go alone and look the situation over before Jumai joined him. He went to Kano and spent some time with the church leaders in the open sections. He lived at the mission and went into the city each day to scout out the situation. Each day was full of caution and prayer as he began his strategic task. The wrong move or even the wrong word might close the doors against him. Thus Adamu walked into the city, sat down and chatted quietly with the *malams*, who were not in the least hesitant to share their learning. They often discussed the Old Testament Scriptures, with which most *malams* were familiar. Adamu would turn the discussion to blood sacrifices, and deftly guide their thoughts to the New Testament and the supreme sacrifice for sin made once for all.

After several weeks, Adamu brought his family to Kano. The next step was to find a house.

The old section of the city, known as the *birni*, was divided into small sections, with a headman over each section. During Adamu's daily visits to the *birni* he had become quite well known. One *malam* especially had become friendly. Since this *malam* was also a headman, Adamu approached him about buying a house in his section. The *malam* was surprised by the request, but told him he would let him know if he heard of a place for sale.

There happened to be in this section a plot of ground on which there was no building. It was reported to be the haunt of evil spirits, and no one would build there. At one time a man had purchased a piece of ground on this plot and started to build. He died suddenly. The half-finished building was cleared away and the plot sold to another unsuspecting person. The new owner also started to build and died before the house was finished.

The *malam*, who was friendly but not particularly sincere, had an idea. Why not sell the land to Adamu? He would certainly die, as had his predecessors, and that would put an end to his preaching. The next time the *malam* saw Adamu, he showed him the property.

Adamu went home to tell the church leaders, who suggested that they pray about it for a week before taking action. Others joined them in prayer. At the end of the week Adamu took several Christians with him, and together they had a look at the property.

The *malam* told them that the former owner was in the southern part of Nigeria, but he would contact a "brother" who lived in the city. Four days later, a bargain was made. Adamu knew that he must not give the impression of having ready money, or the price would soar. So the plot was paid for in the slow, traditional fashion. Three months after he first inquired about a house, Adamu walked home with the deed in his hands.

The building began while Muslim neighbors looked on, expecting Adamu to drop dead at any time. The building was finished, the house was plastered inside and out, and Adamu was still very much alive.

"Well, the day he moves into the house, he will die," prophesied the neighbors.

A few days before Adamu and Jumai moved in, one of the *malams* took Adamu aside and told him all that had happened in the past. "And now," he warned, "when you move into that house, you had better call a group of *malams* together, have them make a sacrifice, and pray to Allah for your protection. That place is a place of demons."

"My God is greater than the demons," replied Adamu confidently. "If I follow Him with my whole heart, the demons cannot touch me." The *malam* went away shaking his head.

Adamu, Jumai, and Musa moved in. One lone Christian family, the only light in that dense spiritual darkness. One little Christian home in the midst of 90,000 people who were hostile to the gospel.

11. The Inner City

Living among Muslims was a life to which Adamu was
accustomed. For Jumai it was entirely new. Her
widowed mother and elder brother had become Christians when she was very young, so that she had known
only the warmth and security of a Christian home. She
had grown up in a large Christian community. Now she
found herself, a mere girl, several hundred miles from
her Christian friends, surrounded by women who would
not even communicate in a friendly way. Nishama had
been difficult, especially in the early months, but the
inner city of Kano was openly hostile.

Many men in the neighborhood had the four wives allowed them by Islamic law, and as many concubines as they could afford. Jumai soon learned that the women were rarely allowed out in the streets, and were not to be seen in the public market places. Their main contact with the outside world was visiting across the mat fences which separated the compounds. They might, after dark, slip through the fence and visit a neighbor's house. Thus shut up, unable to read, rarely hearing outside news, and with much free time on their hands, these frustrated women's minds and mouths were filled with evil.

While Jumai's heart ached for these women, they in turn were amazed at her. She walked freely in the streets. She sat and talked with her husband and did not seem afraid of him. And her baby! She fondled him in front of people and even called his name in public. They, according to custom, pretended shame for their first-born. They showed him no love, nor mentioned his name in public. Nor did they include the first-born when they counted their children.

"But why be ashamed of the child God has given you?" Jumai asked a group of her neighbors one day.

The women shrugged their shoulders, but answered with a note of pride. "It is the custom we have inherited from our parents and grandparents. We follow our custom."

When the women saw that Jumai did not do *salla*, the five-times-daily Islamic prayers, they openly showed their contempt by referring to her as "heathen."

And so, expecting her second child, Jumai sat alone

in her house day after day while Adamu went out among the people.

It was here, alone, in the walled section of Kano City, miles from friends, that their second child was born. Adamu darted back and forth, making meaningless suggestions about going for help.

"The mission is too far away," Jumai moaned between pains.

"Then I will call in the neighbor women."

"They hate me. They will not help. No, Adamu, you must bring your child into this world. Lock the door."

The door was locked, and, following his wife's directions, in due time a dazed Adamu found himself with a slippery, screaming infant in his arms.

"What shall I do with it?" he asked, alarmed.

"Hold it, while I bathe myself," his wife told him calmly.

Even though they now had that pride of all African communities, two young children, one an infant at the breast, the hostile attitude of their neighbors did not change.

Open persecution, in fact, soon followed. Since the demons had not molested Adamu and his family, the people reasoned that they must take a hand themselves. One day Adamu found a little bundle of fetish "medicine" that had been thrown into his compound during the night. Having himself used such medicines before he became a Christian, he knew the demon power behind them. Uneasy, he showed the bundle to a Christian friend. The friend advised him to burn it, reminding him that God was mightier than any demon power.

After some days, Adamu found another charm that had been thrown into his compound. Examining it, he found that this was one intended to make him insane. Again he took it to his friend, and again the friend had prayer with him. The fetish was burned, and Adamu went back to his little family. The neighbors were perplexed when they saw that no harm came, but they were not prepared to give up.

One morning when Adamu opened the front door, he found that blood had been smeared on the threshold and evil "medicine" sprinkled over it. Had he stepped on it with his bare feet, the poison it contained could have killed him. He went back into the house and prayed for protection. Then, taking a torch, he burned the bloodstained place and swept the ashes away.

"Fetishes. Poison. Hatred. Oh, Adamu, I live in fear," Jumai cried to her husband one day.

"I know," Adamu attempted a comforting tone.

"Not for myself," Jumai continued. "I have been hated before. But the children. They do not look where they are walking. They might be killed, and for no reason."

"God must be our reason," Adamu stated quietly. "His will, His message must be our reason. And whatever happens to us or our children, we must follow our Lord's direction."

"I know what you say is right, Adamu. And I know you say it with as much feeling for our children as I have. I will pray for strength."

All this time Adamu did not cease to witness quietly to any one who would listen. It was never easy, and more than once he was driven out of a compound. Children were told to throw stones at him—stones which resulted in more than one deep scar.

Jumai continued trying to find a key into the hearts of the women. They shunned her as an unclean thing. She tried different ways to get into their homes, and finally gained an entrance by asking one of them to teach her to weave. Through this she was able to make several friends, and in time some of the women ventured in at her door. These women were consequently shunned by the others. The battle was hard and long, but Adamu and his little family felt happy in each other's love, and secure in the Heavenly Father's keeping.

They witnessed with heavy hearts the celebration of Islam's "big" *salla*, or day of atonement, which was held annually, and for which thousands upon thousands of people flocked to Kano.

White rams, their long hair washed clean, were taken to a large open field, and while thousands looked on solemnly, the head Islamic teacher offered prayer over the sacrifices. Small holes had been scooped in the ground to receive the animals' blood after their throats were cut. The ceremony completed, each worshiper filed past, dipping his finger in the pool of blood, hoping to find special merit in the world to come.

Dressed in flowing white robes, the worshipers stood side by side like a mighty army, facing Mecca. In unison and in plaintive tones they repeated the creed: "There is no God but Allah! God is great!" The sound of their voices was like the roaring of the sea, and the picture they presented like its waves, as the worshipers fell down on their knees, then prostrated themselves, their foreheads touching the ground, three times in slow succession.

After more prayers, the crowd dispersed to enjoy the festivities of the parades, feasting, and debauchery.

Adamu knew from his own past experiences that their hungry hearts were still hungry. "Has the big *salla* brought you peace?" he asked his neighbor.

"We cannot know until after death whether Allah has accepted us or not," the neighbor replied sadly.

As the two lonely Christians knelt to pray that night, deep in the walled city of Kano, they thanked the Lord again for the forgiveness they had found through the shed blood of the Lamb of God.

12. The Visitor

The long-legged passenger being bounced along in the old truck was facing a problem. He was on the way to his old home. Since leaving his people as a boy of 15, Adamu had not been back to see them. How should he greet them?

During the years, he often thought of his family: his old uncle, Amadu, who had been opposed to his returning to school; his four older brothers; his boyhood friend, Ibrahim.

"Are they still alive?" he wondered. "How will I identify myself? How will they feel toward me after all these years?"

He knew he could not just walk in and say, "I am your lost brother." They would not believe him. The Fulani were far too suspicious of strangers to accept such a statement. He must do or say something that would make them recognize him. He prayed and planned.

Thus it was that he arrived as a stranger in the little village. He walked along its narrow, winding paths, memory guiding his footsteps. Things looked strangely familiar, unchanged even after many years. Before long he found the compound which he recognized as his old home.

He paused at the door and called his greetings. He was told that the man of the house had gone out but would be back shortly. He sat down in the shade of a tree to wait, the same tree under which he had played as a boy. Amadu, whom Adamu immediately recognized as his uncle, arrived in due time. After the formal salutations, Adamu, speaking in Hausa, the trade language, asked if he might stay the night.

The old man looked suspiciously at the loads the stranger had brought with him—two boxes, a roll of bedding, and a bag of books. "I do not take in Hausa traders," he parried. "But there is a place in the Hausa section where you might find lodging."

"But I would like to stay with you," Adamu persisted.

The uncle brought the usual excuses: the houses were crowded, the wives were not well, and unable to cook food. But Adamu would not take no for an answer. He sat under the tree, waiting for something to happen.

Men came home with the cattle and sat down to eat and drink. He recognized them as his brothers, and heard them discussing him in the Fulani language, telling Amadu under no circumstances to take him into the house. "He's probably a thief. He'll be gone in the morning, together with your money."

The day was waning and still Adamu had made no contact. "Lord, show me what to do," he prayed.

Suddenly two of his brothers started an argument about one of the cattle. Their voices became more and more heated. Angry words flew back and forth until finally they drew their knives. Neighbors rushed in trying to separate them. Adamu saw his opportunity. He grabbed paper and pencil from among his belongings, and stood facing his angry brothers. "Armed rioting," he stated coldly. "I'm going to report this to the police at Kaduna. What are your names?"

As if by magic, the quarrel ceased. Old Amadu found his tongue first. "You and your stupid quarreling," he said to the brothers, in Fulani. "See what you've brought on yourselves? This man is a plain-clothes policeman. Now what shall we do? We haven't even offered him food, much less a place to sleep. You've got us into something now."

Turning to Adamu, he invited him into the entrance hut and tried to persuade him not to take the words to Kaduna. They offered him food, but Adamu refused, pretending to be offended. There was much uneasy talk which Adamu pretended not to understand. They decided among themselves that they would offer him five pounds as a bribe, and began collecting the money from their friends.

When the excitement had died down, Adamu spoke to his uncle. "I met a man in Kaduna," he began, holding up a pen and paper, "who used to live here. When he heard I was coming this way, he asked me to inquire about certain people."

Referring to the paper, as if the names were all written down, he began with his father's name, Musa.

"Musa?" asked the uncle, as if trying to remember. "Oh yes, that was my grandfather who died years ago. I never knew him myself, but I've heard the elders in the village talk about him."

"Amadu?" asked Adamu next.

"He, too, has been dead for many years," said the uncle, referring to himself.

Adamu then gave his oldest brother's name and was told that he, too, had been dead for many years. As he went down the list of his brothers, most of them were reported dead.

Then he came to his own name. "Adamu Gani," he said. "Is he still alive?"

"Adamu Gani has been dead for some time; we had the mourning for him years ago. He went away from home," said the uncle.

"Did he die away from home?" queried Adamu.

"Yes," said the uncle. "He went into the world and died in the world. We never saw him again.

Adamu sat down again, silently watching his relatives and listening to their conversation, which now was mostly about himself. He recognized some of the neighbors and also his friend, Ibrahim. How he longed to talk with him! Suddenly Adamu pricked up his ears. Ibrahim was speaking. "That man reminds me of someone. Do you know who I mean?"

There were various guesses, but Ibrahim was not satisfied with any of them. He waved them all aside and said, "He looks like Adamu Gani. Do you suppose it could be he? I would like to ask him."

There were shouts of protest. "If you ask him, of course he'll say he is Adamu Gani. Then he'll take some evil advantage of us."

"I'd like to ask him," said Ibrahim, stubbornly. "And if any harm comes of it, I am willing to take the consequences."

Adamu silently thanked the Lord for this answer to prayer, and waited for the question. It was some time before Ibrahim could pluck up enough courage.

After a long wait, Ibrahim seated himself close to Adamu and said, "I have a question I'd like to ask you. I wonder if in all your travels you ever met a friend of mine. He left here years ago and has never come back."

"I have been in various places; I may have met your friend. What was his name?"

"He may have changed his name, but here in the village he was the one you asked about—Adamu Gani."

"I am Adamu Gani," said Adamu carefully.

"Please do not mock me," said Ibrahim. "I would very much like to hear news of my friend."

"*Min Adamu Gani*," said Adamu, and poured out a torrent of information in his mother tongue. Ibrahim fell on Adamu's neck and burst into tears. Then the brothers rushed in and embraced the long-lost one.

The women, hearing the commotion, thought the mysterious stranger was carrying their husbands off to Kaduna, and started to wail. The neighbors heard the wailing and came running to the rescue with knives and clubs. They dropped their weapons at the door when they saw the rejoicing. Adamu's baggage was brought into the house. There was now more than enough room for him.

They sat under the stars that night to talk. Adamu spent much time telling his relatives and neighbors of his travels, his experiences, and of the one great experience of God's forgiveness in Jesus Christ. They agreed that something remarkable had happened to him. "A Muslim would never come back just to visit."

Thus Adamu brought the gospel to his family. He spent two weeks with them, explaining God's plan of salvation and answering their questions and objections. There was no open response, but he won their friendship, and when he left them to return to Kano it was with peace in his heart.

13. The Riot

In Kano City the Christian home continued to be a light in its dark surroundings. Adamu's little family grew to four, then five, and then six. Seeing no harm had come to Adamu, others, too, became bold enough to build on the land surrounding Adamu's house. Soon their neighbor's houses were all around them, like boxes in an untidy storeroom.

Although persecution continued to be strong, five of the *malams* who were Adamu's most powerful enemies died during the first eight years that Adamu lived in the *birni*. One of the more friendly *malams* said to him, "You must truly be a man of God. The men who sought to do you harm are dying one after the other."

For many years there had been strained feelings between the Hausas, who lived in the walled city, and the Ibos and people from other southern tribes who had come to Kano to pursue their business. This enmity smouldered beneath the surface of the city's activities, usually showing itself only in minor incidents—personal clashes and disputes. It was a serious factor, however, and from time to time erupted in major conflagrations, one of which precipitated a mass exodus of Ibos, and created political hostilities which in turn led the nation into the civil war of 1967.

While living in the inner city among the Hausa people, Adamu and Jumai were caught up in one of the outbursts that plunged the entire city into terror. It began one day when a Hausa wanted to buy from an Ibo. The Ibo made a derogatory remark. Bitter words led to a fist fight. Soon the Hausas gathered to help their fellow tribesman. The Ibos rushed in to help their brothers. The brawl grew until the police had to intervene. They were able to restore order, but the affair was by no means settled.

In the walled city that night a quiet announcement was passed among the Hausas. "Prepare your weapons. Tomorrow we go out of the city to fight the Ibos."

Silently through the night weapons were prepared. Bows and arrows, knives, machetes, clubs—everything that came to hand.

The next day, Sunday, Adamu started out on his bicycle to attend an early meeting at the mission several miles away. His wife and children would follow later for the morning service.

He had not left the walled section when he found himself surrounded by an angry mob. He said to them, "I am a Christian and a preacher of the gospel. I have nothing to do with this trouble."

But the men were angry and refused to listen. He was about to be carried away by them when some of the crowd recognized him and eventually he was released. He continued on his way, unaware of the extent of the disturbance.

The chief of Kano, alerted to impending trouble, rushed police to all the gates of the walled section. He was too late. Many of the Hausas had already left, and many more evaded the police by climbing over the walls into the Ibo section. The riot was on.

At the mission, the church service finished and there was still no sign of Adamu's family. Knowing that they had been on the way to church, Adamu became apprehensive. He started home, but was stopped by a policeman. "It's too dangerous to go any farther," he was told.

"But my family—they are in there!" insisted Adamu.

"You cannot go in. You will have to watch and wait."

The Hausas had attacked the Ibos with hatchets, machetes, and clubs. They broke down the walls of their little shops and entered the living quarters. Some were taken by surprise in their sleep and killed in their beds. Their goods were dumped into the streets, and plundered. The Ibos fought back with guns, killing men, women, and children alike. But no one would touch a

baby, and more than one woman saved her own life
by holding her baby in front of her as a shield. Bodies
were dragged through the streets as a warning to others.
Corpses were covered with grass, drenched with gaso-
line, and set on fire.

Realizing the terror that had been unleashed, Adamu
was filled with fear. Where was his family? Eventually
troops arrived from Kaduna and restored order by
threatening to shoot anyone who refused to go home.
Fifty people had been killed and the loss of property
was devastating.

And Jumai? When she and the children had reached
the gate that morning, they had been stopped by a policeman. "You will be killed if you leave," they were told,
and they were forced to turn back. But where was her
husband? All day long she waited, but all the news she
heard was of fighting and bloodshed. By five o'clock
there was still no word of Adamu. She concluded that
he was killed. The fear that had held back tears during
the day lost its hold. First Jumai, and then the frightened
children wept. Then, through her tears, Jumai saw a
man enter her door. And, although the tears continued,
the weeping turned to laughter as Adamu held her in
his arms.

Later that evening, in the uneasy stillness of the inner
city, Adamu gathered his family around him and read
his favorite Psalm: "The Lord is my shepherd; I shall
not want . . . . Yea, though I walk through the valley of
the shadow of death, I will fear no evil: for thou art
with me; thy rod and thy staff they comfort me."

14. In Green Pastures

During his years in Kano, Adamu spent many weekends in the Fulani villages surrounding the city. Through his efforts many of these people accepted the gospel and little groups of Christians met to worship each Sunday. To these Pastor Adamu had the joy of ministering. With results inside the city virtually nil, those groups of believers from among his own people were a great source of encouragement and satisfaction.

Then came an invitation for him to go on a two-month evangelistic trip among the thousands of Fulani in the neighboring country of Dahomey. Adamu readily agreed. At that time a French territory, Dahomey lay along Nigeria's western boundary, thrusting northward from the ocean almost to the Sahara. Adamu traveled several hundred miles west and south by train and truck, watching the countryside grow progressively greener and more luxuriant. The mosques became more infrequent, the influence of Islam less pronounced. On and on he traveled, passing, it seemed to him, into a different kind of world. One thing remained certain—he would find his own people, the Fulani, almost everywhere he went. A nomad tribe, the Fulani built new camps whenever shortage of grazing land for their cattle made it necessary. They would stay in a camp several years, or leave after a few weeks. In Dahomey, the Fulani were found among at least 10 of the more distinct tribal areas.

But there was a difference in their attitude. Adamu, accustomed to the indifference and antagonism of Kano. was hardly prepared for the friendly reception that awaited him.

His two months in Dahomey were to be filled with experiences which God would use to alter Adamu's life.

At Nikki, his first stopping place in Dahomey, he was met by a missionary who had come to escort him the rest of the way. The white man spoke neither Hausa nor Fulani. At one stop on their journey, the missionary had some business to attend to. Trying to be helpful, he thrust French paper money into Adamu's hands and indicated by sign language that Adamu should buy himself something to eat.

Adamu looked at the pieces of paper and stuck them into his pocket. He felt very much a stranger in this land. Reaching the market place, he sat down under a tree and listened to the people speaking. He understood nothing. Hardly realizing it, he said aloud to himself, "Here I am. I'm hungry, but no one can understand my language. I have money, but it means nothing. Lord, help me understand this money."

He had scarcely finished his prayer when he heard a voice in his own tongue, asking, "Friend, what would you like?"

Surprised, Adamu looked up into a kindly face. "I'm hungry," he said. "And I don't understand this money."

"Let me see your money," said the stranger. Soon the money was explained and the food bought. And, to Adamu's surprise, he learned that although the people spoke to each other in their own language, nearly everyone in the market could also understand Fulani.

While Adamu ate his guinea-corn cakes, he told his new friend why he had come to Dahomey. The stranger listened with growing interest. Suddenly he jumped up. "Wait!" he said, and the next moment was lost in the crowd. When he returned it was with a group of men. "I want them to hear, too."

Adamu was taken from place to place in the village, and was asked over and over to tell the story of salvation. Adamu could scarcely believe the interest that they showed. Surely this was a harvest field, ready to be reaped!

In the town of Parakou, Adamu was met by a missionary who spoke Fulani. Adamu was given a place to stay, and in a day or two they began their campaign. Together the two traveled from village to village on bicycles, preaching and teaching as they went. Adamu was surprised that here the Fulani were not Muslims as they were throughout Nigeria, but pagans who worshiped evil spirits. Adamu had many contacts with them as he visited different tribal areas. Many distant memories were painfully revived as Adamu saw the shrines outside the Dahomian villages.

He was often asked during the two months which was the right way, Christ or Islam. He visited districts where Islam was already a strong influence. In other villages the Roman Catholics had established schools and were attracting the people. But every place Adamu and his companion went, there was eager response. Ears were willing to listen and hearts were ready to receive.

In one large town the chief refused them permission to speak. The people, as well as Adamu and the missionary, were disappointed. When they reached the outskirts of the town, Adamu halted and began singing in Fulani, "Into my heart, come into my heart, Lord Jesus." Immediately a group of children gathered. Soon the older men and women stopped to listen. In almost no time he had a large audience. The Fulani love to sing.

Someone suggested, "Let's go into the town, so more people may hear."

"The chief has forbidden us in the town, but the open fields belong to God. I will speak to you here," said Adamu.

The news of the meeting reached the chief. "We are learning a very sweet song," it was reported.

The chief sent a messenger to ask Adamu and the missionary to come into town. When the men reached the chief's place, followed by a large crowd, Adamu said to the chief, "We wanted to preach, but you refused."

"I was afraid you would ask for a gift," the chief explained.

In a matter of minutes a large crowd gathered. They listened intently to Adamu's message. The chief insisted that they spend the night, and he himself invited the people for another meeting that evening. During that gathering the chief publicly acknowledged his faith in Jesus Christ.

The following morning the two men taught the new converts some verses of Scripture and a few choruses, and then prepared to leave. The chief accompanied them to the edge of the town to bid them farewell. "Just think what I almost missed," were his parting words.

When his two-month visit ended, it was with great reluctance that Adamu pulled himself away from Dahomey and went back to Kano. He left behind him several hundred converts and scores more who were interested.

During the long train ride back to Kano, he tried to find the answers to his persistent questions. "Who is going to instruct and encourage these babes in Christ? What about the hundreds of children? What will they be taught? Will it be Christ or Islam? Who would go to the thousands of Fulani in the grasslands, who followed their cattle day after day and yet had never heard, even once, of that Great Shepherd of the sheep?"

The undershepherd sighed and watched the scenery speeding past. It seemed to be tearing at his very soul.

What was this sensation? Was God trying to tell him
something?

Years ago, when he was a student at Kagoro Bible
School, Adamu had dreamed of multitudes of souls
going to a Christless grave, and he, though young in
faith, had felt a great urge to go and tell them of One
mighty to save. He had not been disobedient to that
vision. He had lived and preached among pagans and
among Muslims of many tribes. In a spiritual sense he
had followed his tribal pattern, moving from place to
place to care for his flock. A nomad for God, he had
been an obedient and careful shepherd. Most of his
camps had been in dry and barren land, and none so
bleak as Kano, but now he had seen green pastures in
Dahomey. He had found his own people, anxious to
hear and believe.

Would the Master Shepherd send him back to them
one day?

15. The Vision Grows

Two years later Adamu visited Dahomey again. This time Jumai accompanied him. Adamu arrived in the country with great expectation. He was not disappointed. Everywhere he went he received a warm welcome. He went from mission station to mission station, working out from each by car, bicycle, and on foot, visiting towns, villages, and camps. In every place he was asked to stay. Many new groups of believers had sprung up since his first visit. New churches had been built. Among the Fulani, too, some had been baptized and churches had been organized. A number had learned to read.

Some of these churches had consisted first of all merely of a grass roof over a framework of poles. As the church grew, a better building was needed. The second church had grass walls and seats made of thick poles laid across two-pronged sticks stuck into the ground. Some groups, however, had even outgrown this stage and had built mud brick buildings complete with mud seats and mud pulpits.

Typical of the Dahomey Christians was Sabe, whose father was touched by the gospel and became the first Fulani convert in Parakou, a large city in the northern district. Sabe's father and a friend had come one day to the missionary to "hear words about God." They had been told that the missionary had these words, and were amazed to hear the story of One who loved them enough to die for their sins.

The next day Sabe's father walked the long distance back again to the mission to ask, "White man, what was the man's name who died for me?"

The missionary repeated to him again the message of salvation.

The following day the old man walked the weary miles again, and when he reached the missionary's door, he said, "White man, I am ashamed of myself, but I have forgotten the man's name again."

This time when he left the mission, Sabe's father walked along the winding path through the bush, repeating over and over again—"Jesu, Jesu, Jesu."

Among the people won to the Lord through this man's testimony was his oldest son, Sabe. Sabe came out boldly for the Lord, but the followers of Islam were bidding for his young life too. When he built a new house, the Muslim *malam* told him to build a charm into the wall or lose the blessing of Allah. Sabe bought a charm and built it into the wall. Then he was told that he must sacrifice a sheep before he moved into the house or certain calamity would overtake him. Then he was asked to sacrifice another sheep, and another, until his flock had nearly all been killed. And the more Sabe did the *malam's* bidding, the farther from God he seemed to be.

"Do something," said his grieved father to the missionary. "He is a Christian, but he cannot break with the old ways."

But every time Sabe saw the missionary approaching, he disappeared. At last his father persuaded him to go to the missionary for a talk. When the ladies at the mission saw him coming, they slipped into a room to pray. For two hours the men talked and read the Scriptures, until the whole story came out—the fear that made him hide the little charm in the mud wall, the fear that made him sacrifice sheep after sheep, the unhappiness in his heart.

With the missionary's help Sabe saw Jesus as the One who could free him from fear. The wall was torn down; the charm burned. And as Sabe entered more and more into the freedom of Jesus Christ, the scorn of past friends and the intimidation of the Muslim leaders became an exercise of faith rather than fear.

On this return visit, Adamu rejoiced to find Sabe a leader among the Fulani Christians.

There were other Fulani families just as promising,

under just as much pressure, and just as eager to learn. But the missionaries were far too few to help them all. The work in Dahomey was still young, and there was foundational work to do—reducing languages to writing, preparing primers, translating the Scriptures, teaching school, and ministering to the sick.

Adamu saw that, more than anything else, these young Christians needed to be taught. "They must learn to read and grasp the Scriptures for themselves," he told Jumai. He visited one area where a whole group of young Christians, unable to read and with no one to help them, had turned to Islam. "Do not the Muslims, too, pray to God?" they countered.

As Adamu traveled about, he saw little churches that had been erected in the hope that someone would come to minister. Some of these churches had stood empty, waiting, for over a year.

The great need was for trained Fulani—true shepherds who would be willing and able to feed the Lord's Fulani flock. Fulani believers now numbered in the hundreds, but there were other thousands who had not yet heard the name of Jesus.

Yes, a Bible School was the answer, a Bible School for the Fulani, taught in the Fulani language.

16. Through the Shadows

Adamu and Jumai returned from Dahomey, and continued their quiet witness in Kano City. But Jumai sensed in Adamu a restlessness. He often spoke of the need of his people in Dahomey and their eagerness to hear and know the Word of God.

Adamu and Jumai had been in Kano City for 11 years. Several men and women from among their neighbors were now attending church services at the mission. Since this meant traveling several miles, it showed genuine interest, if not in the message, at least in the messengers. But there were no openly confessed believers in Kano's inner city.

Then Adamu developed throat trouble. It was not
thought to be serious at first, but the pain and loss of his
voice necessitated his spending time in the government
hospital from time to time. His condition did not im-
prove. A black shadow began to form around the little
home. Eventually, after a bad attack that put him in
the hospital for six weeks, the doctors gave their verdict:
"We can do nothing more for him. He is going to get
progressively worse, until he dies."

Hearing this, a concerned missionary doctor arranged
for Adamu to enter a mission hospital. While he was
there, word was sent to the pastor and church leaders at
his beloved Kagoro. They soon initiated plans to bring
the family home to Kagoro from Kano. There was a
mission hospital at Vom, less than 100 miles from
Kagoro, where Adamu could rest and undergo treatment. The children could be settled in school at Kagoro.
Jumai could spend her time between the five children
and her husband, wherever she was needed more.

There was no alternative; the Christian family moved
out of Kano. The lighthouse was closed. None heeded
the sad little procession that carried the pastor's few
belongings out of the inner city. To the human eye the
11 years of struggle and heartache had ended in failure.
For hundreds of years Islam had held sway in Kano
City. Each succeeding generation had passed on the
teaching to its children and its children's children. Even
as the small group carried Pastor Adamu's things
through the streets, the followers of Islam began the
first *salla* of the day, prostrating themselves to the east
and praying in the name of Muhammed.

When the sick pastor reached Vom hospital, he could hardly speak above a whisper. He was given strict orders not to use his voice. From his bed in the crowded ward, Adamu surveyed the pathetic condition of those around him. The look of death was on several faces. "They must hear," he thought, and opened his Bible. His voice rasped loudly enough to be heard throughout the room.

In the midst of his message Adamu became conscious of someone beside him. Turning, he looked into the face of the doctor. The doctor smiled and said nothing, but wrote something on the patient's chart. Presently a nurse came in with a needle, and for several days the preacher was too sleepy even to open his eyes, much less his mouth.

Adamu led five souls to the Lord during his seven weeks at Vom. And in spite of the fact that he used his voice to testify for the Lord, he steadily improved. The doctor now felt that rest and nourishing food were his most important needs, and Adamu was permitted to return to his family.

Among the tall mahogany trees, at the foot of the beautiful Kagoro hills, surrounded by Christian friends, Adamu rested. By the end of the year he felt well enough to enroll in the pastors' refresher course at the Kagoro Bible School. Jumai enrolled in the Women's Bible School.

As the school year drew to a close, Adamu wondered about his future. Nigeria had just become an independent nation. While the people as a nation understood the meaning of independence and accepted the role solemnly and graciously, there were many individuals

for whom it meant casting off all restraint and doing as
they pleased. The new word, "freedom," was on every
tongue.

Adamu spent occasional weekends ministering in the
surrounding churches, and Saturdays often found him
among the Kagoro hills, visiting the Fulani camps.
Often he wanted to ask for a pastorate in this large
Christian community, but he could not forget his own
people, three to four million Fulani scattered throughout northern Nigeria and Dahomey.

It was just a week before the close of school and still
Adamu had no definite plans for the future. Then a
visitor appeared in Kagoro and asked to see Adamu.
The pastor was delighted as he recognized one of the
missionaries from Dahomey.

"Would you like to come to Dahomey when you have
finished school?" the missionary asked. "If you and
your wife would come, there would be much work for
you among the Fulani."

17. The New Path

Jumai brought hot water for her husband's bath. She hesitated for a moment at the door before she spoke. "I shall go with you," she said quietly.

Adamu raised his eyebrows, crinkles of delight creasing his eyes. "You have decided?" he queried, knowing as he said it that the question was unnecessary.

"Yes, I shall go to Dahomey with you. I could not sleep all night. The Lord was speaking to me."

"You have considered the children?" asked Adamu. "We can take only little Ruthie with us. The others will have to stay here for schooling. We won't see them for three or four years."

"I've thought of that," answered Jumai. "The Lord will take care of them."

It had been a hard decision for her, and she had needed time to think and pray. To leave her beloved Kagoro home, her own children, her friends, and travel to another country to live among the Fulani was the hardest thing she had ever faced—much harder even than Kano. Adamu had not hurried her. If God had called him, He would call her, too. Now Jumai had made her decision.

"Praise the Lord!" said Adamu, jumping to his feet. "We can go to Dahomey as missionaries, and work among my Fulani."

Nearly a year had passed since the first call had come, and Adamu felt he should delay no longer. Leaving Jumai to dispose of their household goods, he bade good-by to his friends and his children, and started out on the long journey.

Three months later, when Jumai gave her farewell message in the Kagoro church, she calmly read three verses from her Bible.

"Go ye into all the world and preach the gospel to every creature."

"And the things that thou hast heard of me . . . the same commit thou to faithful men who shall be able to teach others also."

"Preach the word, be instant in season and out of season."

Then she said good-by to her many friends, four of her five children, and her aged mother, and set out to join Adamu in Dahomey. Ahead of her lay a new path in a country of strangers who spoke a strange language. "The call of God does not always appear pleasant," she mused as the miles flashed by her train window. God was asking her to step into an unknown situation, but she knew that He was at her side, and she was content.

Adamu and Jumai were in Dahomey nearly a year before Adamu's dream of a Fulani Bible School began to take shape. A site was obtained at Tchatchou, near Tchaourou, and building began. With customary whole-heartedness he threw himself into the work, seeing, at last, his vision being realized.

The students came from many parts of Dahomey. Most of them were sent by the people of their own villages, with the intent that after learning, they would come back to teach them. So the students came, bringing their wives and families with them. The school was to be their own responsibility as much as possible, with aid from the mission only as necessary. Working together, they built their houses in a cluster, with an open court in the center.

A small community farm worked by the students and their families supplied some of their food. The rest was miraculously supplied, week by week, mainly by the churches. Adamu would smile as he told visitors, "It is an amazing thing. No one has had to leave school for lack of food. No one has gone hungry."

The Bible School was not just Adamu's project. It was a venture in team work, with his wife playing an important role in the partnership. Jumai soon found her hands full. First of all, she knew, her home must be a pattern for the many Christian homes which would be

established in the years to come. Her life must be a
gracious invitation to the women around her. And,
following her example, women only recently out of the
darkness of paganism would learn to train and discipline
their children. Although she could speak no Fulani, she
acted, and what she did knew no language barrier.

Adamu was the only person with whom she could
converse. With a new baby tied on her back and a toddler
by her side, she undertook teaching women who gathered
in the classroom. At first she used sign language. But as
months slipped into years, she learned to speak Fulani.

She taught classes in hygiene and infant care. She
started a sewing class where women with awkward fingers
learned to use a needle in making clothes for their
children.

When new babies arrived in the homes of the students,
Jumai was there, helping and teaching how to care for
the mother and the babies. Often she would say to the
women, "When you go back to the bush, you will need
to know how to help other women in childbirth."

There was one tribal custom which Jumai worked
especially hard to break. The Fulani, like many Muslims of Nigeria, were ashamed of their first-born. From
his birth to the day of his death, a mother would not
show any love for her first-born child. She would not
speak the child's name. If dared to throw the child into
the bush, or put it down in the middle of the motor
road, she would do so, leaving it until someone else
picked it up and returned it to her.

Often as Jumai talked to the women about this
custom, they would answer, "We do not care about

ourselves, but our people will never forgive us if we do not carry on this custom." To break with tribal custom would mean a break with family and friends.

At one time a woman who had no children enrolled in the women's class. The woman, who had taken the Christian name Rebekah, had learned to read and had a bright Christian testimony. Her husband, too, was a Christian, but was too busy with his cattle to attend Bible School. The couple longed for a child to complete their home.

Jumai's heart ached for Rebekah, and she often prayed for an orphan baby to place in this childless home. Then she heard of a baby whose mother had died shortly after its birth. Arrangements were made. At a public ceremony in the church, Jumai brought the baby and placed her in Rebekah's empty arms. There was a prayer of dedication, and Rebekah tied the baby on her back. The infant immediately cuddled down and went to sleep.

Rebekah had a baby to love, the child had a mother and father of her own, and Jumai had an opportunity for teaching the women a practical lesson in caring for infants.

18. Fulfillment

For Adamu, the Fulani Bible School was an answer to the prayers of many years. He felt in it a sense of fulfillment that knew no bounds. It was as though the nomad had at last found rest, a place to live and serve and put down roots.

His was the privilege of teaching the Word to his own people in their language. These young students were his children in the Lord. They would carry the torch when he could no longer do so. Adamu's heart was at rest as he taught.

He translated his favorite Hausa hymns into Fulani.

He drew maps of Paul's journeys. He made free translations of the Scriptures to use in teaching.

There were memorable experiences, too. One of the most exciting was the day a missionary on a motorcycle rode up to Adamu's door and proudly handed him a little book. Adamu gave one look, hugged the book to his breast, and shouted, "It's come! Praise the Lord! It's come."

Waving the book in the air, he ran toward the students' compound shouting, "Come and see! It's here! It's here!"

The students poured out of their homes and gathered around Adamu, shouting in delight. Eagerly they examined it—the first copy of the New Testament in Fulani. The result of long months of painstaking labor by missionary linguists, the first shipment had arrived from the British and Foreign Bible Society. The missionary brought a bundle from his bike, unwrapped it, and presented each student with a copy. It was a highlight in Adamu's life, a thrill that never wore off. Now his people had the Word in their own language—the Fulani Scriptures for the Fulani nomads.

As time passed, the school grew and the work prospered, but not without opposition. The chief of the Fulani in Tchatchou did not like Adamu and his students. "You are killing our religion," he told them.

The chief tried to drive them out. From time to time his cattle "accidentally" got into the small school farm during the night. He stirred up other Fulani to hostility.

But Adamu continued teaching and the students continued preaching. The Fulani chief decided he must do something drastic. Word was passed along, and bows and arrows were prepared.

Coming out of the classroom one afternoon, the men noted with alarm that the compound was being surrounded by an armed mob. A messenger approached, warning them that the first man who ventured out of his house would be shot. The students met in a little hidden group to pray.

Adamu ran to his house, his mind in turmoil. His life had been threatened many times before, but only he and his family had been involved. This time the Bible School students were threatened. What would happen if one of them should be killed? Would the Bible School be broken up? What of the future of the Fulani work?

"The Lord is my shepherd." Of course! The thought calmed him. Everything would be all right. Was not the Shepherd watching over *all* the flock? There may be danger, but the Shepherd knew about that, too. Gathering his little family about him, he read from the Word: "Yea, though I walk through the valley of the shadow of death, I will fear no evil, for thou art with me; thy rod and thy staff they comfort me." His favorite Psalm had been read often in times of danger. He prayed, committing the students and their families to the Lord's keeping. Then he waited.

After a few hours, there was an unexpected movement among the mob. Voices rose and fell. Arms waved. To Adamu's delight the would-be killers began leaving. They scattered as quietly as they had come. Adamu earned later that the Bariba chief in Tchatchou, a very influential leader, had sent a message to the Fulani chief saying, "You dare not touch these people. They have brought only good to our village. If you harm any of them, you will answer to me!"

Opposition did not cease immediately, but it decreased noticeably, and with the passing of time the Fulani chief accepted the school as a fact of life.

19. The Lord Is My Shepherd

The months sped by, turning into years. Adamu and Jumai became respected leaders in the Fulani church. The believers looked to them for guidance and teaching, and many considered them their parents in the faith.

On their twentieth wedding anniversary Adamu and Jumai were given special recognition, a token of the esteem in which they were held. National Christians and missionary friends were invited to share with Adamu and Jumai in food and fellowship. It was a happy time, with singing and prayer and a message from the Word.

When the day was over and the friends had gone, Adamu was left alone with his thoughts. He had taken his chair outside. Myriads of stars twinkled in the tropical sky.

One little daughter was asleep on his lap, the other nestled against his leg. He thought back over the past 20 years. It had been best to let God choose. What a true helpmate Jumai had been to him, praying with him and for him; encouraging him when he felt downhearted; steadying him when his impetuous nature wanted to rush into things; making a home for him and his children—a home where he always felt free to invite his friends.

He thought of his other children far away in Kagoro. Musa, his first-born, would soon be graduating from teacher training college. The others were progressing in their schoolwork, too. He thought about Kagoro. Kagoro was where he had met Jumai, Kagoro was where he had spent happy years in Bible School. It was while working on the railroad near Kagoro that he had first heard the message he now preached, and had given his life to Jesus Christ.

His thoughts took him to his old home in Bornu. He sat again, a little boy with freshly-shaved head, sitting astride a donkey on his way to Koranic school. He heard again his father's voice, as if it were yesterday, saying, "Your brothers can look after the cattle. You are my fifth son, my little Dembo. It is my desire that you become a servant of Allah."

Adamu unfolded his long frame from his chair and picked up his children. God's ways were often strange, he mused, as he started back into the house. But they were always true, always right, and always best. He glanced once more at the starry sky and smiled to himself as he crossed the threshold. "The Lord is my shepherd," he said softly. "I shall not want."

20. Epilog: The Nomad Finds Rest

After four years in Dahomey, Adamu and Jumai went back to Kagoro for a furlough. It was arranged that Samuila, a graduate of the school who had some experience in teaching, was to look after the school in their absence.

Adamu and Jumai received a warm welcome from their many friends in Kagoro. A house was provided for them near Jumai's mother, and they were happy to be together again with their family. But they were restless, nonetheless, at being away from their work in Dahomey.

Whenever they were asked to speak in churches, the

burden of their message was the Fulani work, the many who were still without Christ in Dahomey, the ones who were begging for a teacher to come and live in their villages, the ones who had even built churches, hoping that someone would come to them.

But when their furlough time was up, the door for their return seemed to be closed. Jumai's aged mother was now very frail, and Jumai felt that she should not leave her. Adamu himself was not well. Periodic attacks of dysentery left him weak and exhausted.

One day he went to the Mission in Jos to visit Effie Varley, a missionary friend of many years, who had suffered a heart attack. Her life had been an inspiration to Adamu, who held her in high esteem.

They visited for a while, and when Adamu rose to leave, Miss Varley took his hand to say good-by. Looking at him earnestly she said, "Adamu, there is no greater honor in this world than to be called to the Lord's work, and to be faithful in that work."

Even as she spoke, her heart gave its final beat, and she passed into the presence of the Master.

This made a great impression on Adamu, and unwell though he was, he longed more than ever to be back in his school in Dahomey.

Then one day word came that Samuila had been called to another place of service, and the Fulani Bible School was to be closed. Adamu and Jumai talked long that evening. "I will go alone," Adamu said, "while you stay with your mother."

"But I do not like to think of you going when you

are not well," Jumai demurred. "I will not be there to take care of you. How will you get your food?"

"I have thought of that," Adamu replied. "I will ask Rebekah and her husband to move near the school so I can eat with them. God has always taken care of us," he continued. "Is He not the Shepherd? I have said before, Jumai, and I say again, that when death comes I want it to find me busy in the Lord's work."

And so Adamu returned to Dahomey, leaving Jumai to care for her mother and the children. He was received warmly, and eagerly resumed his teaching.

One morning, after he had been back only a short time, he led the little household in early morning prayers as usual. But a little later, Rebekah found him lying down. He complained of dizziness and headache, but insisted that he would be all right.

At the school, when it was time for classes, the students waited in vain for their teacher. He did not come. They went to investigate, and found him in great distress, vomiting blood. Immediately they sent word to the missionaries, and preparation was made to take him to the government hospital in Parakou, about 25 miles away.

Adamu begged to be left at the school. "There is no medicine that can help me now," was his plea. "Do not take me away. I want to die here." But there was no alternative. The hospital was the only hope of adequate treatment.

Adamu was taken gently to Parakou, and word was sent to Jumai in Kagoro, although it was impossible, they knew, for her to come to him.

It was his final illness. A week later, on April 28, 1967, Adamu Dogon Yaro, God's messenger to the Fulani, quietly passed away. Peacefully, but triumphantly, he entered the green pastures, and the glorious presence of the Good Shepherd.

The next day his friends gathered on the grounds of the Bible School. Together they read from the Fulani New Testament and sang a hymn. Together they bowed in prayer. Then they laid to rest the body of their friend, and placed a wooden marker above the grave. They prayed once more, and sang another hymn.

Then they dispersed, not to sorrow as those who have no hope, but to await the great day of resurrection and their glad reunion with Adamu, and Jumai, and God's Fulani, and all the saints, to offer praise to the One who loved them, and to dwell in the house of the Lord— forever.